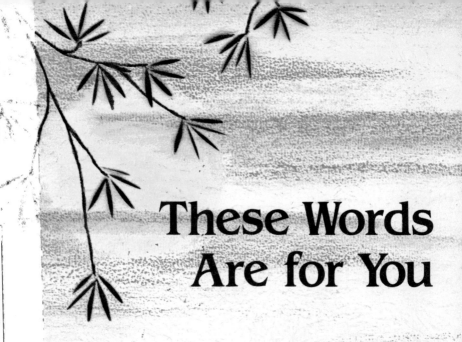

These Words Are for You

by Leonard Nimoy

These Words Are for You

Other books by

Blue Mountain Press INC.

Come Into the Mountains, Dear Friend
by Susan Polis Schutz
I Want to Laugh, I Want to Cry
by Susan Polis Schutz
Peace Flows from the Sky
by Susan Polis Schutz
Someone Else to Love
by Susan Polis Schutz
I'm Not That Kind of Girl
by Susan Polis Schutz
Yours If You Ask
by Susan Polis Schutz
Love, Live and Share
by Susan Polis Schutz
The Language of Friendship
The Language of Love
The Language of Happiness
The Desiderata of Happiness
by Max Ehrmann
I Care About Your Happiness
by Kahlil Gibran/Mary Haskell
I Wish You Good Spaces
Gordon Lightfoot
We Are All Children Searching for Love
by Leonard Nimoy
Come Be with Me
by Leonard Nimoy
Creeds to Love and Live By
On the Wings of Friendship
You've Got a Friend
Carole King
With You There and Me Here
The Dawn of Friendship
Once Only
by jonivan
Expressing Our Love
Just the Way I Am
Dolly Parton
You and Me Against the World
Paul Williams
Words of Wisdom, Words of Praise
Reach Out for Your Dreams
I Promise You My Love
Thank You for Being My Parents
A Mother's Love
A Friend Forever
gentle freedom, gentle courage
diane westlake
You Are Always My Friend
When We Are Apart
It's Nice to Know Someone Like You
by Peter McWilliams
It Isn't Always Easy
My Sister, My Friend

These Words Are for You

by Leonard Nimoy

Blue Mountain Press ™

Boulder, Colorado

Library of Congress Number: 81-68585
ISBN: 0-88396-148-2

First Printing: November, 1981
Second Printing: March, 1982

Thanks to the Blue Mountain Arts creative staff,
with special thanks to Faith Hamilton.

Photos by Stephen Schutz

Blue Mountain Press INC

P.O. Box 4549, Boulder, Colorado 80306

CONTENTS

Introduction

Leonard and Sandi Nimoy

I was moved to tears on an airplane recently. It caught me completely by surprise. We had been flying for an hour or so on a cross-country flight. I was staring out the window when suddenly I became aware of a young lady standing in the aisle. She leaned over and said simply, "Thank you for many hours of pleasure." Then she was gone. I turned to the window and wept.

Why? Why this sudden surge of emotion? I have been complimented before. I have been applauded, bravo'd and cheered at after performances before innumerable audiences. I've also had my share of critical jabs, but that's another story. I have been gratified by the sounds that an audience uses to let an actor know that his work is appreciated. Yet there was something different, special . . . . . in that moment on that plane. Yes, the statement was heartfelt, but many others have been equally sincere.

Now, sometime later, having had time to examine the experience, I suspect it was the element of surprise. The totally unsolicited, surprising quality of the compliment, the gift which moved me so deeply. There was no negotiation, no discussion, no expectation or obligation. It was an open-handed/asking nothing in return, surprise gift.

We all negotiate. Actors work hard in a performance and expect applause in return. It is an honest bargain. "I'll do my share, you do yours."

We treat people well, hoping for, or expecting decent treatment in return.

We acknowledge the "special days." Birthdays, anniversaries, Father's Day, Mother's Day, etc. All well and good, but these are negotiated and anticipated communication.

I'm convinced, because of my startling personal experience, that the smallest unexpected kindness can have a lifetime impact.

Now I enjoy taking an occasional moment to call someone when I don't owe a call, to send a note that isn't required, and to give a hand of friendly help when it hasn't been requested or expected.

It is still a kind of "bargain" or deal, but one that I make with myself. I do get something in return. I've discovered that when I do it, it makes me feel very good!

I never saw her again. I don't even know her name. Yet, I've always been grateful to that young lady on the airplane. With a few words, she extended herself to me in a way so personal and so generous that my life has been forever enriched. I'm hopeful that this book will help me to pass on her gift.

Her words were for me . . .
"these words are for you."

These words are for you
To have,
To hold
To keep from now on
Forever.

I love you,
Need you.
I need your laughter
I need your love
Need your warmth

Because,
I care about you
and
I love you

Someone
I'm always delighted to see

   Someone
      Who is welcome
      to what I have

   Who offers
      what I need
   Before I even realize
      I need it . . .

Who takes
  easily and gratefully

Who gives
  for the joy
    of it

Who doesn't need
  to keep score

That's you

  my friend

You and I have had our share
of laughter
and our share of sadness
our share of good and bad times

and we have our share
of those sweet and precious times
when we seem to blend
into one being
and I am so filled with happiness
that my eyes overflow

some would say these times
are stolen moments

I disagree

I think we've worked for them
I think we've earned them

*For the times
When I said things
I shouldn't have
    I'm sorry*

*For the times
When I did things
I shouldn't have done
I ask you to
    Forgive me*

*I find no pleasure
In giving you pain
It makes me feel better
To make you feel good.*

When you
　　Let me take
　　　I'm grateful

When you
　Let me give
　　I'm blessed

I *came to you*
  Lonely and
   Drifting . . .

You taught me
  What I'm worth

I came to you
  Hungry
   And I was fed

I came to you
  Needing
   And you gave

When I talked,
 When I spoke
 Of my yearnings
  And my dreams . . .
You listened,
 And not only listened
  You heard.

    Will you let me
      do
     the same
    For you?

*L*et's do it
   All over again
   Starting from
   The beginning

   Let us re-touch
      Every step
      Along the way

All the joys, fears
   Laughter and tears
   That brought us as
            close
   as we are
            Today
Let's do it all

            All over again

You and I
have learned
The song of love,

And we sing it well

The song is ageless
Passed on

Heart to heart
By those
Who have seen
What we see
And known
What we know
Passed on by lovers
Who sing
With us now
And lovers who have
Sung before
Our love is ours
To have
And
To share

The miracle is this
The more we share...
The more
We have.

I'll be with you
         soon

To share
  The seasons
      passing

The crisp of fall
The bud of spring

I'll bring
    You

Kisses,
  Caresses . . .
    Aged by timeless longing

Eye to eye
  Hand in hand
    We'll whisper
        softly
Of Our Love

Away and alone
I fill the room
With thoughts
   Of you
   And other times
   In green fields
      Of love remembered
      And cherished . . .

What shall I send you
Across the sea?
   A moment of sweet silence
   Reaching to soul depths
      In hopes of touching
      Your being
         With my mind

I send you this
   My love
These words,
   These special words
   To warm you
      While I'm gone

      Take them to you
      Hold them
         In your heart

My love is for you
   My love is you

      Take these secret words
      That open doors
         To sacred places
            Known only by lovers
            Such as us.

You are my ground
You are my base
My island

You are my safety
And my warmth

You are my harbor
With you I am safe
And at peace

I can be social
And make small talk
But the truth is,
I'm shy

You are my haven
And my retreat

I may act secure
And self-assured
But I'm human . . . .

I have my moments
Of self-doubt
And I can be hurt
Just like anyone else

You are my firm ground
You are my strength
You are
my love.

YES

Is scary . . .

> *It's so final*
>> *So full*
>> *So complete*

NO

Is easy . . .

> *It closes doors*
>> *And windows*
>> *It hides facts*
>>> *And problems*

NO . . .
> *Is an end.*

But,
> *YES . . .*
> *Is a beginning*
>> *A pledge*
>> *A promise*
>>> *A commitment*

>> *To you*
>> *My love,*
>>> *I say YES.*

I *know*
That there is nothing
In this world
That you wouldn't do
If I asked you to
And I would do
The same for you

I love
To see you
Play the child...
  Alive
    Excited
      Hopeful
        Dreaming...
  Forever
    The optimist
  Forever
    Entranced
    By a new thought
      A new idea...

      I hope
      That I can go on
      Forever touching
      Those ideas
      That awaken
        The child in you

I don't touch you often enough
I don't tell you often enough
That I care about you.

If I were to take the time
To tell you about each time
That I think of you,
I would spend
All my time
Telling you about
Thinking of you

How indifferent
How uncaring I must seem
  When I see the tear
  That tells me
  You've been hurt
    By me or others
    Or some long forgotten
    Pain
      Which rises up again
      To hurt you once again

If
  I seem withdrawn
It's only because
The pain that hurts you
Hurts me too
      So deeply . . . .
      Because,
        I care about you

There have been times
When I thought
    I've seen it all
    I've done it all before.

And yet tonight
    When I saw the sunset
It felt so new
So . . . first time

And now,
    When I see again
    In your eyes
    Your love for me
I'm as touched
    As I was
    When it all began

    Some things
        Bear repeating.

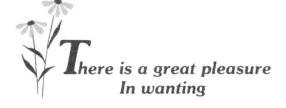

There is a great pleasure
In wanting

The object of desire
Seems so perfect
so useful
so necessary
You wonder how you
Ever got along without it
And you know that you must
Have it now

Closets full of neglected,
Once desired objects
Tell me that
It was the wanting
That was important

I have learned
A precious lesson

I have learned
To want
What I have.

I love to sit with you
　　At dusk
　　To watch the day
　　　　Withdraw . . .

Night is coming
But,
　Before it does
　A crack opens
　　Like a doorway
　　Between two worlds

　Hand in hand
　We slip inside
　　Travelling through
　　Unknown reaches
　　　On voyages of wonder

　　Weightless . . .
　　We leap and bound
　　Over magic mountains
　　　Through soft mists
　　　　Into rich purple valleys
　　　　Flying free
　　　　　Toward the horizon

　　In a moment
　　We have lived
　　A lifetime

　　　Returning
　　　　Just in time
　　　　To ease through
　　　　　The doorway
　　　　　As night closes

Soft . . .
　The dream of you
　　Steals across
　　My sleep
　And whispers
　　Wake to me
　　Wake
　　　to
　　　　me

I whisper back
　Your love
　And we sing
　　Our song
　　　Silently
　　　　Secretly

Until the morning light
　　Tells us
　　　It is time

I awake
　Fulfilled
　Stirring from
　　Our night dream
　　　To begin
　　　　Our daydream

I have seen
the beauty of love
in your face

I have met
the joy of existence
in your being

I have found
the eternity of life
in your presence

I have touched
the fulfillment
Of perpetual grace

And it is you
all of it
is you

My heart
goes out
to the lonely

For I have been alone

My heart
goes out
To the lost
For I have been
weary
aching of heart
Yearning
for sharing
and comfort

As long as there
is you
then there is us

As long as there
is us
I can never be
alone

I wish that
it were so
for all

And my heart goes out
to the lonely

I'm not always able to give

    I'm sometimes empty

And even when
    I want to give
    Sometimes I can't find
    The key to the door of me

And even when I get
    The door open
      Sometimes
      There's nothing there

So please understand
    When I can't give.

In a little time
    I'll be full again

I love to give
    And as soon
    As I can
        I will

When I am working hard
At something I love
Time goes too fast

When I am doing something
I am not happy doing
It takes forever

When I'm waiting for you
Time goes too slowly

When I'm with you
    Time disappears

*W*hen I see
The sorrows of the world
Leaning heavy
On your shoulders
I wish they were
On mine instead

Because,
I care about you.

If the sun turns cold

If the night is too dark,
    long and lonely

Try me.

If your trust
        has been betrayed

If dreams won't
        come true

            When hopes seem
                to crumble
                and fade
                    to dust

        Try me.

If your sadness
        leaves a void

        An emptiness
            which can't
                be filled
            Except
                by love

                Try me.

Where will
There ever be
A space
So full
As that
Which is filled
By our love?

We are star met
we are joined
we are blessed
we who have found each other
we are the dream of the ages
we are the hope, the desire
we are love

Sometimes
    Are grey times

Scanning
    The overcast sky

    Across the tops
    Of wet stately pines
      I look for the light
        Of heaven's rays

    Blocked by the
        cold grey
        of winter clouds

Until at last
    thinning to fleece
      the moist white
      gives way

    And

      As it has always
        been
      The darkness lightens

    Allowing me
      to see through

      To the first
        patch
          of blue

I *have learned again*
    To trust myself

Sometimes . . .
    It isn't easy

Sometimes . . .
    Someone who seems
        to know
    Someone who seems
        to be wiser
    Can convince me,
        that I'm on
        the wrong path

Not wanting to seem
    too stubborn
Not wanting to be
    too difficult

    And above all
    wanting to be
        liked . . .

I have occasionally
  been persuaded
    to leave my own path
      to go the way of another

  Even when all my instincts
    tell me to trust myself

    Sometimes it works
      but often it doesn't.

  And worst of all

    Sometimes it's hard
      to find my own way again

I *have lived with me*
for a long time
and plan to continue

I would like
to keep my friendship
with others

But,
I must keep faith
with myself

*S*o many times
  I've thought . . .

   I need
   I want
     someone to help me

    Someone to understand
        to care

    Someone or something
       to soothe this emptiness
        this feeling of being lost

  It never works that way

    When I care

    When I help or console
    Or offer understanding
      To someone else

      My own emptiness disappears
      And I am fulfilled

Day after day
            passes
As I wonder
            what next?
What shall I do next?

What shall I begin
            to try
            to do
            to challenge
                    myself?

Finally,
        The answer comes
            simply...
                clearly....

        Do something
            for someone else...
        Some surprise
            something...
        Some unexpected
        something
        Which says,
            I thought
                of you
            I care
                about you
            I wanted
                to do
                    something
                        for you...

I have learned
that there is a time
to trust

As the flower
trusts the bee
which feeds
upon it

There is a time
to take
as the hillside trees
take
the rain
and the sun...

And in the proper season
   just as the shrub
      offers the blossom

And the tree
   offers the fruit

There is a time
   to give

For that
   which is given
      to us
Is to be enjoyed
   enhanced
      and returned

So that others
   may have it
      use it
         and pass on
            what they can

Whatever I have passed on
has come back
to me
in word
and deed

Whatever I have given
I have gained

And now
I shall
start the cycle
again

You mean so much
to me
I wish
I could be
A cushion following you
Wherever you go
To be there
In case you should fall.

I won't do that.

It would deprive you
Of your self-respect
But please,
If there is a bruise,
Let me help to heal it.

It is time
to give
For I have been given
so much

And now it is time
to give in return

I have seen pleasure
and sorrow
triumph
and defeat

I have seen
the joys of life
and watched
the face of death

I have walked
the road
Which sometimes seemed
unbearably long
hard and unbending

I have seen it
suddenly become
a path of glory
rich
fertile
lush
and giving

We started with love
And when our love
Was sometimes shaken
We braced it
With understanding
To give it strength
   And when our dreams
   Were sometimes shattered
   We picked up the pieces
   And carefully put them
   Together . . .

Binding them with patience
And time . . .
We nursed each other
   Through defeat
     And learned
     To be graceful
     In triumph
     And now,
          We are twice blessed
          We are still lovers
             And we are friends

I want to see you again
To hold your hand
To touch your face
To feel the earth stand still again
I want to breathe with you
As one again
Not just now and then
But always

Take these words
For they are yours

Take these thoughts
For what else
Can I give?

What more can I give
Than the thought
That you are
Loved

Take this love
For who else
Could I give it to
But you

Leonard Nimoy